SUSSEX BUSES

JOHN LAW

AMBERLEY

A peek inside Eastbourne Borough Transport's depot in 1977 reveals Leyland Panther No. 2 to the fore, among various AEC and Leyland types.

First published 2018

Amberley Publishing
The Hill, Stroud
Gloucestershire, GL5 4EP

www.amberley-books.com

Copyright © John Law, 2018

The right of John Law to be identified as the Author of this work has been asserted in accordance with the Copyrights, Designs and Patents Act 1988.

ISBN 978 1 4456 5025 8 (print)
ISBN 978 1 4456 5026 5 (ebook)

All rights reserved. No part of this book may be reprinted or reproduced or utilised in any form or by any electronic, mechanical or other means, now known or hereafter invented, including photocopying and recording, or in any information storage or retrieval system, without the permission in writing from the Publishers.

British Library Cataloguing in Publication Data.
A catalogue record for this book is available from the British Library.

Origination by Amberley Publishing.
Printed in the UK.

Introduction

The county of Sussex lies on the south coast of England, with Kent to the east, Surrey in the north and Hampshire to the west. It is mainly rural, though well-healed due to its proximity to London. The South Downs, now forming most of Britain's newest national park, straddle the county west to east. Until recently, there was only one city in Sussex, Chichester, with its Anglican cathedral. However, in 2001 the Queen granted the twin towns of Brighton and Hove city status. Brighton and its surrounding conurbation is by far the largest in the county. Other reasonably sized seaside towns include Hastings, Eastbourne and Worthing. In between and inland there are several small towns such as Rye, Lewes, East Grinstead and Horsham. Close to the border with Surrey is the large new town of Crawley, while nearby is London's second airport at Gatwick.

1889 saw the county being divided into two parts – West and East Sussex. Despite both Crawley and Worthing being larger, Chichester became the county town of the western section. Lewes had control of East Sussex. The government's 1974 boundary changes continued with these arrangements.

From the middle of the nineteenth century, horse buses had been operating in Sussex, but it was not until 1884 that the first tramway opened. This was operated by the Shoreham & Brighton Tramways Company, initially with steam traction, but was later horse-drawn. The route was from Shoreham-by-Sea to Westbourne Villas, Hove, but never got any further into Brighton. Despite being taken over by the British Electric Traction Company (BET), electrification could not be agreed on, so the system closed in 1913.

Brighton Corporation Tramways commenced in 1901, gradually expanding, but ceased operating in 1939, mainly replaced by trolleybuses. Trams began running in Hastings from 1905 until 1927, when trolleybuses took over.

By far the biggest bus operator in Sussex was Southdown Motor Services. Later to become a BET company, the company was formed in 1915 as a result of three firms coming together to offset shortages of staff and materials caused by the First World War. Takeovers saw the company expanding, with its territory reaching Eastbourne in one direction and Eastern Hampshire in the other. The company became famous for its express services and coaching holidays, bringing the green livery to many parts of Britain and Europe.

Southdown became part of the National Bus Company in 1969 and was to take over former Tilling Group operator Brighton, Hove & District. Soon the standard NBC green livery was applied to the company's buses. The 1980s saw great changes, however. A version of the lighter green colour scheme was adopted and Brighton & Hove became a separate company once again. Southdown was sold to Stagecoach in 1989 and that company's stripes soon began to appear. The operations and depots east of Brighton were later disposed of.

In the very east of Sussex, Maidstone & District was the dominant operator, having absorbed the Hastings trolleybus system. The split of the former National Bus Company subsidiary saw Hastings & District reformed, until taken over by Stagecoach.

The northern parts of Sussex, particularly in the Crawley and East Grinstead areas, were once the territory of London Transport's green 'Country' buses. These later fell into the hands of NBC-owned London Country Bus Services. Today, Go-Ahead-owned Metrobus now serve this part of the county.

There were two municipal bus operations in Sussex. Brighton Corporation (and its successors) survived until it was purchased by Brighton & Hove in 1993.

Eastbourne Corporation Transport was unusual in that it never ran trams, as it commenced operations with buses as early as 1903. Throughout its life it had a fascinating selection of vehicles, but all this was to end in 2008, when it was sold to Stagecoach.

The independent sector never had a large presence in Sussex. By the early 1970s, there were very few, with the exceptions of Tillingbourne (in the Horsham area) and Dengate of Rye. Both have since been consigned to history. However, the mid-1980s saw the introduction of deregulation, plus many unprofitable routes were subject to the tendering process, as they were vital to the communities they served. This meant that the smaller businesses were able to enter the stage carriage market. In the long term, many did not survive, but even today some are thriving. In Brighton there is the innovative Big Lemon, with its yellow vehicles, while other companies include Compass Bus, Renown and Southdown PSV.

Today, Stagecoach, Brighton & Hove and Metrobus dominate Sussex, with Arriva vehicles also occasionally being seen. Nevertheless, these operators provide a well-presented and varied collection of buses, while the likes of Compass Bus and Renown add to the scene, making Sussex a great place for any bus enthusiast to visit.

Thanks to Trevor Hall, Steven Hughes, Peter Tuffrey, Jim Sambrooks, Richard Huggins, the late Les Flint and Bus Lists on the Web (www.buslistsontheweb.co.uk) for assistance in the production of this publication.

Brighton's 3-foot, 6-inch gauge tram network opened in 1901, with fifty four-wheeled open-top cars. A typical scene, in London Road, Brighton, shows car No. 36, *c.* 1910. Trolleybuses were later introduced and fully replaced the trams in 1939.

Tramway operation in the Hastings area began in 1905, but it was not until 1907 that the two separate sections were joined. Electrification along the seafront was by the Dolter stud contact system, which was never very successful and dangerous to horses. By 1913, cars on the seafront service, like No. 43 shown here, were fitted with a petrol engine, but this did not work too well either. Overhead wires on the seafront were finally allowed to be erected in 1921. Therefore, this view of the Parade in Hastings must have been taken before then.

Trolleybuses began operating in Hastings in 1928, quickly replacing the trams. A fleet of Guy BTX three-axle vehicles was initially employed, one of which, No. 6 (DY 4968), is seen in the company of an unidentified local bus in Hastings town centre, c. 1930.

The Hastings trolleybus system finally closed in 1959, but one trolleybus was kept by the operator, by then Maidstone & District, as a heritage vehicle. Dodson-bodied Guy BTX No. 3 (DY 4965) was fitted with a diesel engine and was thus able to attend rallies and other special events. It is seen posed outside Silverhill depot, Hastings, in April 1908, photographed by the late Les Flint.

The early years of the twentieth century saw motorised transport introduced to the roads of Sussex. One of the earliest operators was Sussex Motor Road Car Company, established in 1904. One of their original double-deck buses, registered CD 393, is seen posing outside the Lamb Inn in Angmering, a Lambert & Norris of Arundel house. That brewer was taken over in 1910 and became part of Friary Meux (later Ind Coope), while the bus company was merged with others to form Southdown Motor Services.

An early motor bus that has survived into preservation is this Milnes Daimler open-topper registered D 1999, restored to its Brighton & Hove livery. It is seen on Brighton seafront on 2 May 1976, having completed the Historic Commercial Vehicle Club Rally from London.

The large seaside town of Worthing never had a tramway; however, it did have the 'Tramocar'. A small fleet of Shelvoke & Drewry Freighter buses, with low floors suitable for the elderly population, was introduced in 1924 by the Worthing Tramocar Company. Here is an example, registered PX 1592, outside the Pier Hotel on the seafront in Worthing.

The Worthing Tramocar Company was bought out by Southdown Motor Services in 1938. Yet it is still possible to ride on a Tramocar, as one has been built on a genuine Shelvoke & Drewry Freighter chassis, with a replica body. It is a regular performer at the Amberley Chalk Pits Museum in West Sussex and BP 9822 is seen operating there in summer 2002.

Southdown Motor Services was the principal bus operator in Sussex, at least until the National Bus Company was dissolved around 1990. Part of the British Electric Traction Group (BET), it came to have a large fleet of Leyland buses. An early example is No. 0135 (CD 7045), a Leyland G7 of 1922 with a Short Bros body built in 1927. The bus had been retained by the company as a preserved vehicle and is seen at Scare Hill, north of Brighton, on the London–Brighton rally in the South Downs in 1967.

1943 saw Southdown take delivery of a batch of Guy Arabs with 'utility' bodies, thirty-three of which were later cut down to open-top. They were used on summer routes at most of the seaside towns, including Hayling Island, Eastbourne and Brighton. It is at the latter resort that we see No. 447H (GUF 147), a Guy Arab II with fifty-six-seat Park Royal bodywork, which had been converted to open-top in 1950.

The Guy Arab obviously found favour with Southdown as more were purchased in the 1950s. No. 547 (PUF 647), a Guy Arab IV with fifty-nine-seat Park Royal bodywork and fitted with platform doors, was withdrawn by Southdown in 1970. It was purchased by Confidence Coaches of Leicestershire and was sold for preservation in 1973. It is seen, having returned to Sussex, in Eastbourne in early 1986.

Southdown's fully fronted Leyland PD3 type double-deck buses were always known as 'Queen Marys'. They lasted well into the 1970s and several were preserved. Back in 1974, No. 920 (6920 CD) is seen at Southdown's premises in Eastbourne, still in pre-NBC colours, though with the new style fleet name. This Leyland PD3/5 with Northern Counties FH39/30F bodywork had been new in 1962.

Several of the 'Queen Marys' had bodies that were convertible to open-top configuration. No. 409 (409 DCD) was found in its summer guise in Eastbourne in 1974. This Leyland PD3/4 sixty-nine-seat bus was delivered to Southdown in 1964.

Some of the 'Queen Marys' had Northern Counties bodywork with a curved windscreen, such as No. 257 (BUF 257C). This Leyland PD3/4 had a seating capacity of sixty-seven passengers. Southdown was quick to apply the corporate fleet name and double arrow symbol, but retained the pre-NBC colours for much longer. No. 257 was found in that condition one evening in Bognor Regis depot *c.* 1975.

A visit to Southdown's Bognor Regis premises one evening, sometime around 1975, found No. 1166 (166 AUF) parked in the yard outside. This Leyland Leopard with Weymann forty-nine-seat bodywork had been new in 1963. Like the depot at Eastbourne, Bognor Regis doubled as a bus station, giving the public access.

Southdown did not stick exclusively to Leyland Motors for its bus requirements. The early years of the 1970s saw deliveries of Daimler Fleetlines. The first batch had Northern Counties bodywork, while the second had bodies built in Suffolk by Eastern Coach Works (ECW). An example was No. 391 (XUF 391K), which is seen one evening inside Chichester depot, still in pre-NBC livery, c. 1975.

Southdown's green coaches were a familiar sight at tourist resorts throughout Britain and Europe. No. 1786 (HCD 386E), however, was found much closer to home, in Chichester depot, c. 1975. This Leyland Leopard had coachwork by Duple (Northern), seating just forty-one passengers.

The mid-1970s saw standard NBC green paintwork applied to the Southdown fleet, as seen on 'Queen Mary' No. 973 (973 CUF), a 1964-built Leyland PD3/4 with Northern Counties sixty-nine-seat fully fronted bodywork. It is seen under the canopy of Brighton railway station, sometime around 1975.

At this point it is perhaps pertinent to take a look and Brighton, Hove & District (BH&D), a former Tilling Group company that was to be merged with its bigger neighbour, Southdown, in 1969. About ten years before that, BH&D No. 375 (CPM 17) was photographed by the late Les Flint at the Old Steine in Brighton. This 1945-built Bristol K6A, originally bodied by Park Royal, had received a new ECW body in 1954.

Moving forward to 1974 and Southdown No. 8 (OPN 808) is seen at its Old Steine terminus, still in full BH&D red-and-cream colours, and without any sign of NBC (or Southdown) ownership. This Bristol LDS6B Lodekka with ECW sixty-seat bodywork had been new in 1959.

When Southdown took over BH&D in 1969, the livery and identity was retained for a few years, even to the extent of painting Southdown vehicles into BH&D red. An example is that of No. 2108 (PUF 208H), a Daimler Fleetline with dual-doored Northern Counties bodywork, which is seen at Brighton's Old Steine in 1973.

An all-over cream livery was employed on BH&D's open-top buses, including those that were convertible, such as No. 2043 (XPM 43). This ECW-bodied Bristol FS6G is seen in its winter guise at the Old Steine in 1974. The NBC influence is clearly in evidence, as the fleet name is now 'SOUTHDOWN-BH&D'.

Southdown No. 544 (LFS 296F) was photographed at the Old Steine in 1974, in NBC green livery with 'SOUTHDOWN-BH&D' fleet names. This ECW-bodied Bristol VRT/LL6G had been part of the swap between the National Bus Company and the Scottish Bus Group and had originally been numbered AA296 in the Eastern Scottish fleet.

Returning to Southdown's main fleet, it is 1975 and we are inside Eastbourne's Cavendish Place depot, which doubled as a coach station. Proudly standing in a prominent position is this towing bus, numbered 0198. This had been converted from a 1938 Leyland TD5, registered EUF 198. It was later destined for preservation.

Southdown's main terminus in Brighton was a cramped location called Pool Valley, close to the Old Steine and the seafront. Vehicles were always backed in to the loading area and were thus nicely photographable. In this 1976 view single-decker No. 233 (KUF 233F), a Marshall-bodied Bristol RESL6G, is alongside 'Queen Mary' No. 300 (FCD 300D), a Leyland PD3/4 with Northern Counties bodywork.

One of the later 'Queen Mary' Leyland PD3/4 buses, No. 359 (HCD 359E), with a Northern Counties body featuring large windows, is seen at Eastbourne railway station on a rail replacement service in 1977.

For further double-deck requirements, Southdown turned to the Leyland Atlantean, a typical example being illustrated here. No. 727 (PUF 727M) was delivered in 1974 and was an AN68/1R with Park Royal seventy-three-seat bodywork. It is seen in Pool Valley, Brighton, *c.* 1975.

Here is No. 2080 (JPM 80D), another double-deck bus photographed sometime around 1975. This Bristol FLF6G/ECW seventy-two-seat bus had been new to BH&D, but is seen in Southdown NBC colours, with the BH&D bit of the fleet name painted out. The location is Queens Road, Brighton, very close to the railway station.

Sister vehicle to No. 2108 (seen on page 15), No. 2110 (PUF 210H) was found in 1979 in full NBC green livery. This Daimler Fleetline/Northern Counties bus was photographed in the two-bay bus station serving Brighton's main railway station.

Despite being a former BET concern, Southdown liked Bristol buses for some of its single-deck requirements. One such, No. 212 (KUF 212F), a Bristol RESL6G/Marshall forty-five-seat saloon, was found at East Grinstead railway station in spring 1979. Southdown also once had a fleet of Leyland Leopard saloons.

The Northern Counties-bodied Daimler Fleetlines ordered by Southdown for longer distance work were fitted with just the one doorway. No. 379 (TCD 379J) is an example, seen on a very dull and damp day in Horsham town centre in early 1980.

It looks like it has been raining in Brighton in 1981. Seen at its Old Steine terminus is Southdown No. 61 (UGF 61S), a 1977-built Leyland National with forty-four-seat dual-doorway layout. It will shortly depart on a local journey in the direction of Hove.

The 700 route from Brighton to Portsmouth is a long established bus service serving the major communities on the south coast. It still runs today, in the hands of Stagecoach. Back in 1981, Southdown No. 257 (JWV 257W), new in the previous year, is seen at Pool Valley, Brighton, awaiting the long run into Hampshire. Many of Southdown's Bristol VR type buses were fitted with two doors, but this VRT/SL3/6LXB has single-door ECW bodywork.

Very few NBC concerns had two-door Bristol VR double-deckers, City of Oxford, Bristol Omnibus and Southdown being the major exceptions. One of the latter's examples is seen here on a cold but sunny day in 1985. No. 602 (TPN 102S), a VRT/SL3/6LXB with ECW eighty-seat body, is one of those that were convertible to open-top. The location is the Old Steine in Brighton.

For coaching and express duties Southdown used mainly Leyland Leopards, such as No. 1266 (LWV 266P), which is seen in Hastings in 1981. This forty-seven-seat Plaxton Supreme coach is wearing a special livery for Townsend Thoresen Holidays.

No. 2213 (originally 600) in the Southdown fleet, registered TCD 600J, one of many Bristol RESL6L saloons with ECW bodywork, is seen at its Old Steine terminus in Brighton in 1981. This dual-doored thirty-seven-seat bus was being used on local services.

Like most NBC subsidiaries, Southdown was obliged to take Leyland Nationals into its fleet. Unusually, this one had been obtained from its neighbour, Maidstone & District. As Southdown's No. 143, GKE 501L was found in central Burgess Hill, operating the town service in May 1984.

Southdown took delivery of both Mark 1 and 2 varieties of Leyland Nationals. One of the latter, No. 129 (RUF 429X), a 1981-built forty-nine-seat bus, is seen in Pool Valley, Brighton, in 1986. Note the short-lived fleet name, 'Southdown West Sussex'.

As early as 1981 Southdown was showing signs that it wanted its heritage back. No. 1283 (RYJ 883R) has had its NBC corporate fleet name crudely painted over and a more traditional identity applied to its dual-purpose livery. This Leyland Leopard with Duple Dominant Express bodywork was photographed in central Brighton.

By 1986 a version of the pre-NBC colour scheme had returned! Branded as a 'Southdown East & Mid-Sussex' vehicle, No. 1349 (MAP 349W), a Leyland Leopard/Plaxton Supreme Express forty-eight-seat coach, is seen in Terminus Road, Eastbourne, in March 1986.

The registration 407 DCD was originally applied to one of Southdown's 'Queen Mary' Leyland PD3 double-deckers, but was later given to Leyland National 2 No. 137. Originally registered as RUF 437X, the bus is seen in West Street, Chichester, in autumn 1989. The registration plates were later noted in use on a Stagecoach Alexander Dennis Enviro saloon.

Another second-hand Leyland National in the Southdown fleet was No. 53 (VOD 603S). It had been new to Western National in 1978. In its new colours, it is seen in the village of Newick, north of Lewes, in 1990, actually in the hands of Stagecoach, but with no obvious sign.

One of the last buses to be delivered to Southdown as an independent company was No. 303 (F303 MYJ), a Volvo Citybus B10M-50 with Northern Counties bodywork featuring seventy-six coach seats. It is seen in Queens Road, Brighton, in late 1989. By then Southdown had become part of the Stagecoach Group, and that story is told further into this publication.

In preparation for privatisation, the Brighton area operations of Southdown were formed into a separate company in 1985, to be called 'Brighton & Hove'. A red-and-cream livery was soon adopted, but at first buses ran in NBC livery with appropriate fleet names, as illustrated by this 1986 view of Leyland National No. 3 (BCD 803L) at Pool Valley, Brighton.

In National Holidays livery, with Brighton & Hove fleet names, is No. 1011 (A811 CCD), inherited from Southdown. This Leyland Tiger/Duple Laser fifty-seat coach is seen in North Street, Brighton, in 1986.

Proudly wearing its new colours is Brighton & Hove No. 571 (GNJ 571N), a 1974-built Bristol VRT/SL6G with ECW seventy-four-seat bodywork, which is seen waiting to turn right out of Old Steine and into North Street in summer 1986.

Brighton & Hove No. 157 (C457 OAP) sits in the sun at Pool Valley in Brighton in 1986. This forty-nine-seat Leyland National 2 had been new to Southdown a year earlier.

One of the first vehicles delivered new to Brighton & Hove, No. 406 (C376 PCD) sits at Pool Valley, Brighton, in summer 1986. Branded for the 737 express service to Heathrow and Windsor, this Plaxton-bodied Leyland Tiger, seating fifty-one-passengers, had been received by Brighton & Hove in March.

Like many operators in the 1980s, Brighton & Hove turned to the minibus for certain operations. Though it had been initially delivered to Southdown, at the end of 1985, No. 203 (C203 PCD) soon received its red-and-cream colours. The Mercedes L608D/Alexander twenty-seat vehicle was found parked on the seafront in central Brighton in 1986.

Minibuses did not find favour everywhere, and Bournemouth Transport soon got rid of theirs, to the advantage of Brighton & Hove. No. 357 (G57 BEL), a Mercedes 7811D/Wadham Stringer, new in 1989, is seen at Brighton railway station in 1990.

The privatisation of Brighton & Hove occurred in 1987, with a management buyout. The company's vehicle purchasing policy soon began to differ from that of Southdown. Some of the first double-deck buses new to the company were Scanias, such as this N112DR with East Lancs eighty-seat bodywork. No. 708 (E708 EFG) is seen at Portslade railway station in 1989. Brighton & Hove became part of the Go-Ahead Group in 1993.

In 1997 Brighton & Hove absorbed the former municipal operator Brighton Blue Buses. From that source came No. 126 (XFG 26Y), a forty-nine-seat Leyland National 2, which is seen in its new livery opposite Brighton station in autumn 1997.

Brighton & Hove No. 71 (M71 CYJ), which previously carried the same number in the Brighton Blue Buses fleet, is seen at Brighton railway station in autumn 1997. This Dennis Dart/Plaxton forty-seat bus had been delivered to the council-owned fleet in 1995.

Brighton & Hove purchased its own Dennis Darts, such as No. 4 (N504 KCD), bought new in 1995. With its forty-seat Marshall body, it is seen in North Street, Brighton, just a few months after delivery.

In recent years Brighton & Hove has implemented a policy of naming its vehicles. No. 810 (T810 RFG) is seen bearing the name *Magnus Volk*, the engineer of a pioneering electric railway running along Brighton's seafront. Seen at the Old Steine in March 2003, this East Lancs-bodied Dennis Trident is painted in a livery dedicated to route 1.

Another photograph taken in March 2003 shows Brighton & Hove No. 235 (R235 HCD), which has not yet been named. Seen in North Street, Brighton, it is a Wright-bodied Volvo B10BLE seating thirty-nine passengers, and was delivered new in 1998.

Named after theatre critic Jack Tinker, Brighton & Hove No. 860 (Y869 GCD) was photographed in North Street, Brighton, in March 2003. This seventy-seven-seat Plaxton-bodied Dennis Trident carries a route-dedicated livery for 'Metro Line 5'.

Brighton & Hove also imported a few buses from London; No. 31 (NDZ 3161) had been new to London Buses as No. DW161 in 1993. It always carried a Northern Ireland registration, as its body had been built there, in Ballymena by Wright Bus Ltd. The chassis is a standard Dennis Dart. It is seen in Queens Road, Brighton, in March 2003.

Brighton & Hove No. 114 (N414 MPN) was found in Uckfield's small bus station on 23 May 2006, en route from Brighton to Tunbridge Wells. This Dennis Lance with forty-seven-seat Optare Sigma bodywork had been new to the company in 1996.

Seen in suburban Hove on 20 February 2009 is coach-seated Brighton & Hove bus No. 780 (R880 HCD). Typical angular-looking East Lancs bodywork, seating seventy-eight passengers, is carried on a Scania N113DRB chassis.

Brighton & Hove No. 842 (Y868 GCD), a Plaxton-bodied Dennis Trident is seen in Hangleton, a suburb of Hove, high up in the South Downs, on 14 May 2007. The bus is named *Eugenius Birch* after a Brighton-educated architect who specialised in seaside works, including Brighton's West Pier.

Danny Sheldon was a former mayor of Brighton who died in 1982, but his name is remembered and displayed on Brighton & Hove bus No. 618 (GX03 STZ). A convertible open-topper, this East Lancs-bodied Scania N94UD is picking up passengers for a breezy trip up to Devil's Dyke, in the South Downs, from Queens Road, Brighton, on 10 July 2009.

Brighton & Hove No. 54 (YN58 BCO), one of several Scania CK23OUB OmniLink forty-three-seat saloons in the fleet, is seen in North Street, Brighton, on 5 May 2017. It is named *John Peckham*, who is said to be the oldest traceable inhabitant of Brighton, and who became Archbishop of Canterbury in 1279.

Adding a touch of colour to North Street in Brighton on 5 May 2017 is Brighton & Hove No. 426 (BF12 KXA), advertising the delights of Drusillas Park, a tourist attraction near Lewes. This Wright-bodied Volvo B9TL is named *Janet Brown*, an actress who died in Hove in 2011. She was best known for her impressions of Margaret Thatcher.

New to East London Buses in 1999 as No. TA72 (T672 KPU), this Alexander-bodied Dennis Trident was later sold to Brighton & Hove. Here it became fleet number 884 and was named *David Sheppard*, who was a former captain of both the Sussex and England cricket teams. He passed away in 2005. The photograph was taken at the Old Steine, Brighton, on 13 April 2007.

In London the Mercedes-Benz Citaro 'bendibuses' did not find favour and were soon disposed of to the provinces. Brighton & Hove received some for the busy service to the universities. New to London General (part of the Go-Ahead Group) as No. MAL106 (BD57 WDS), it is seen at the Old Steine in Brighton as Brighton & Hove No. 113 on 5 May 2017.

Brighton & Hove's recent double-deck deliveries have been of the Wright 'StreetDeck' design. No. 943 (BX15 ONV), one of the first batch for the 12/12A 'Coaster' service, is seen in Eastbourne on 5 May 2017. It has been named *Alfred Richardson* after a well-known Brighton milkman who served the Kemp Town seafront area when many film stars lived there.

Brighton & Hove No. 803 (SK16 GWE) is an example of a lower-height Wright 'StreetDeck' bus, a seventy-seater with dual-doorway layout. With a higher 'StreetDeck' behind, the differences can be clearly seen. No. 803, named *Martin Langfried* (he sounded the bugle at the Battle of Balaclava and is buried in Hove), is seen in North Street, Brighton, on 5 May 2017.

In the far east of Sussex the dominant operator was Maidstone & District, a BET concern that had inherited the former Hastings Tramway business. As well as the two depots in the Hastings conurbation, a small depot was maintained at Rye. Outside that facility in 1974, with Rye railway station in the background, is No. 3342 (342 NKT), a 1961-built AEC Reliance with dual-purpose, forty-seat Weymann bodywork. It is still painted in the pre-NBC livery, albeit with the new fleet name.

1974 was the year that John Dengate & Son was taken over by Maidstone & District. The company had operated several rural routes out of Rye. In October of that year, ex-Dengate RBM 255J is seen beside Rye railway station still in its original colours, but with obvious evidence of the new owners. At the time this Ford R192 with Willowbrook DP45F bodywork had not been allocated a fleet number, but it later became No. 3255.

Maidstone & District's Hastings area fleet contained several Leyland Panther saloons, such as No. 3117 (LKT 117F). With its dual-doored Strachan bodywork, and still in pre-NBC green, it is seen outside Hastings railway station in 1973.

Another Leyland Panther in the Maidstone & District fleet was number 3067 (JKK 167E). Delivered in 1967 with a Willowbrook fifty-three-seat body, it was originally numbered as C67. It is seen in 1974 in Hastings town centre, having recently received a coat of NBC green paint.

Outside of the Hastings area, Maidstone & District had a large fleet of Leyland Leopard saloons. No. 2610 (OKO 810G) was one of a batch of eighteen fitted with Willowbrook dual-purpose bodies seating forty-nine passengers. It is seen in the appropriate NBC livery inside Rye depot in 1974.

Enthusiasts used to flock to Hastings during the summer months of the 1970s to ride on Maidstone & District's pair of AEC Regal III open-top half-cab saloons. Built in 1946 with a Beadle body, No. 4002 (HKL 826) was photographed inside Hastings depot in 1980 by the late Les Flint, prior to departure on a tour of the historic town.

Maidstone & District received its first batch of sixteen Bristol VRT/SL6G double-deck buses in 1973. A year later, one of them, No. 6684 (HKE 684L), with ECW seventy-seven-seat bodywork, is seen in Hastings town centre while operating a local service.

An amazing survivor in the Maidstone & District fleet was this 1937-built AEC Regal I, originally registered DKT 20. The year 1958 saw it converted to a recovery vehicle and it is in that condition that Les Flint photographed it at Hastings depot in 1980. It has since been preserved.

An unusual vehicle in the Maidstone & District auxiliary fleet was OFN 721F. This former East Kent AEC Reliance/Marshall saloon had been converted to a mobile office and is seen in Hastings as fleet number P145 in 1981.

Maidstone & District's route 900 reached Gatwick Airport in May 1984, when dual-purpose Leyland National No. 3907 (SKN 907R) was photographed there. The bus had started its journey in the Medway towns and travelled via Maidstone, Tunbridge Wells and East Grinstead.

In 1975, as part of a trial by the National Bus Company, Maidstone & District received small batches of Scania Metropolitans, Volvo Ailsas and Series 3 Bristol VRT buses, all based at Silverhill depot in Hastings. One of the Volvo Ailsa B55-10/Alexander seventy-nine-seat buses, No. 5383 (LKP 383P), was photographed at Hastings railway station in 1976.

Maidstone & District No. 5251 (KKO 251P) was one of the seventy-five-seat Scania Metropolitan double-deckers taking part in the trial. Jim Sambrooks photographed it by Ore station c. 1976. Both the Metropolitans and the Ailsas were later moved to Luton depot in Chatham and no further orders were made, though Maidstone & District did later purchase batches of MCW Metrobuses.

In 1980, as part of the NBC's Market Analysis Project (MAP), 'Hastings & District' was introduced as the fleet name of Maidstone & District services in East Sussex. Proudly displaying its new identity is No. 3448 (EKJ 448K). This was one of a large batch of forty-five-seat Leyland Leopards with Marshall bodywork. It is seen in Hastings, approaching the seafront, in 1981.

Also wearing 'Hastings & District' fleet names in 1981 was No. 5131 (WKO 131S), a Bristol VRT/SL3/6LXB with ECW seventy-four-seat bodywork. Fellow NBC operator East Kent had originally ordered it. The location of this photograph is the seafront in Bexhill.

In 1983 Hastings & District became a separate company, in preparation for privatisation. In March 1986, on a misty morning, Leyland National No. 238 (NPD 138L) was found in Hastings town centre, still in NBC green but with the latest style of fleet name. It had been new to London Country in 1973.

On the same dull day as the top picture, Hastings & District No. 370 (VKE 570S) is seen in its new colours in Hastings town centre. This forty-nine-seat Leyland National had been inherited from Maidstone & District, where it had been fleet number 3570.

In March 1986 Hastings & District No. 523 (PKP 123R) was photographed in Hastings town centre about to embark on a journey deep into East Kent territory, ending in the Port of Dover. This 1976-built Bristol VRT/SL3/501 with ECW bodywork had originally been Maidstone & District No. 5123.

After a spring shower in Eastbourne in 1987, Hastings & District No. 156 (GKK 156V) was found loading up in Terminus Road, ready to return home. New to Maidstone & District, it is a Willowbrook-bodied Leyland Leopard built in 1980.

Hastings & District later introduced a bright blue livery, as seen on No. 560 (BKE 860T), a former Maidstone & District Bristol VRT/SL3/6LXB with ECW seventy-four-seat bodywork. It was photographed in Hastings town centre in early 1989, not long before Hastings & District became part of the Stagecoach Group, which will be looked at later in this publication.

Despite the loss of its Hastings operations, Maidstone & District still ran into East Sussex. At Lewes bus station in autumn 1997, No. 3152 (M501 PKJ) is an unusual bus to be operating the 729 service between Brighton and Tunbridge Wells, a joint operation with Southdown. This Dennis Dart with Wadham Stringer dual-purpose bodywork had been new to Kentish operator Wealden Beeline.

The vehicles of the East Kent Road Car Company also made occasional forays into East Sussex. In Eastbourne coach station, operating the 'South Coast Express' in 1975, was DJG 613C, an AEC Reliance with Park Royal forty-nine-seat coachwork. It was later to be rebodied by Plaxton. At the time, East Kent did not use fleet numbers.

After years of standard NBC red, East Kent buses began to revert back to traditional colours in the run up to privatisation, which occurred with a management buyout in 1987. Sometime around 1991, fleet number 1115 (MFN 115R), a Leyland National inherited from NBC days, is seen at Hastings railway station prior to returning to Canterbury. Stagecoach took over East Kent in 1993.

Another NBC operator to run into Sussex was Alder Valley, having inherited services from Aldershot & District. Sometime around 1978, forty-nine-seat Leyland National No. 190 (GPJ 890N) is seen having a rest close to Horsham railway station, and is about to be passed by Southdown Bristol RESL6G/Marshall No. 241 (KUF 241F).

Alder Valley was split up in 1986, into North and South. The latter's fleet name is clearly visible on Leyland National No. 285 (TPE 161S), found loading up in Horsham town centre prior to setting out for Guildford in autumn 1986. Alder Valley South was privatised in 1987, adopting a green-based livery, before ending up in the hands of Arriva. East Lancs Coachworks later converted No. 285 to 'Greenway' standard.

One other NBC subsidiary had a major presence in Sussex – London Country, with garages at East Grinstead and Crawley. It is at the former where we see No. XF8 (CUV 58C), one of a batch of just eight Daimler Fleetline/Park Royal double-deck buses ordered as an experiment by London Transport. All were allocated to East Grinstead and passed to London Country when it took over in 1970. Three of these vehicles, including No. XF8, went to Stevenage between 1969 and 1972 for 'Blue Arrow' services, but had returned to Sussex when the late Les Flint took this photograph on 9 April 1978.

In 1974, Crawley bus station was found to be full of London Country AEC buses. Closest to the camera is No. RCL2233 (CUV 233C), a sixty-five-seat Routemaster with platform doors, intended originally for Green Line duties. In this photograph it has been relegated to the 405 service to West Croydon. Another Routemaster and a pair of AEC Swifts are also visible.

By 1978 London Country's fleet was being modernised and 'AN' type Leyland Atlanteans had joined Crawley Garage's allocation. Branded for 'C LINE' duties in the new town is No. AN146 (UPK 146S), a Park Royal-bodied AN68A/1R, seen at Crawley bus station on a local service.

To assist the NBC in updating the London Country fleet, several AEC Swifts were transferred from South Wales Transport. Several went to St Albans Garage in Hertfordshire, but the rest were sent to Crawley. At the town's bus station in spring 1980 we see No. SMW3 (PWN 703H), with dual-doored Willowbrook bodywork.

Inside Crawley Garage on 9 April 1978 is ex-London Transport No. MBS412 (VLW 412G), an AEC Merlin (the 36-foot-long version of the Swift) with twenty-five-seat, dual-door, MCW bodywork, photographed by Les Flint.

An unusual vehicle in the London Country fleet was No. RN8 (MRR 808K), one of ten AEC Reliance/Plaxton Elite Express coaches acquired from Barton Transport, a Nottinghamshire operator. They were intended mainly for schools duties, but could be pressed into service on longer distance duties, such as the occasional outing to the seaside. Allocated to Reigate Garage (Surrey), No. RN8 is seen approaching the seafront in Brighton in the summer of 1986.

When London Country was split up in 1986, the Sussex operations went to the South West sector, soon becoming known as London & Country, part of the Drawlane/British Bus empire. A pleasant green-based livery was employed, as demonstrated by 'B' type forty-one-seat Leyland National No. SNB538 (EPD 538V), seen in East Grinstead in March 1993.

As an attempt to deter competition in Crawley, London & Country set up a low-cost operation called Gem Fairtax. Seen in that livery at Crawley bus station in March 1993 is Leyland National No. GF313 (AYR 313T). This bus had been new as a dual-doored bus, numbered LS313, with London Transport. London & Country and Gem Fairtax were later absorbed into Arriva, though today Metrobus (part of the Go-Ahead Group) is the dominant operator in Crawley.

Brighton Corporation once ran a considerable fleet of trolleybuses. Most were of pre-war AEC design, typical of this being No. 34 (FUF 34), an AEC 661T with fifty-four-seat Weymann bodywork, built in 1938 for the opening of the system. It is seen, *c.* 1960, at the Old Steine terminus. The system closed in 1961 and No. 34 was sold for scrap. It ended up in a yard at Southerham, near Lewes, where it rotted away until the 1980s. (Les Flint)

On the same occasion as the top photograph, Brighton Corporation No. 63 (FUF 63), again built in 1938, was photographed by Les Flint at the Old Steine, where the Corporation's buses congregated. This AEC Regent I with Weymann bodywork, originally seating fifty-four passengers, later passed into preservation.

In 1958 Brighton Corporation took delivery of twenty Leyland Titan PD2/37 double-deckers, one of which was No. 70 (WCD 70). Fitted with a sixty-one-seat Weymann 'Orion' body, with a rear entrance, it is seen at the Old Steine, *c.* 1960. (Les Flint)

Though the last three photographs were in monochrome, they do show Brighton Corporation's buses in the old style red and cream, a colour scheme shared with Brighton, Hove & District, as they both took part in a co-ordination scheme. The Corporation later adopted a blue livery, as seen on No. 8 (5008 CD), a Leyland PD2/37 with front-entrance Weymann bodywork. It was photographed close to Brighton railway station in 1976, still carrying the Corporation fleet name, though it had become Brighton Borough Transport in 1974.

During 1967/8, Brighton Corporation received a total of seven Leyland Panther Cubs with Strachan forty-three-seat, dual-doorway, bodywork. One of them, No. 38 (NUF 138G), was found in 1974 at the Old Steine terminus. It was later sold to Lockwood's Foods for the transport of fruit and vegetable pickers in Lincolnshire.

Another photograph taken at the Old Steine in 1974 shows one of Brighton Corporation's Daimler Fleetlines, No. 87 (WUF 987K). Painted in a Tesco advertising livery, its Willowbrook body has a dual-doorway layout and can seat seventy-three passengers.

Brighton received some Leyland PD3/4 buses with sixty-nine-seat MCW bodies in 1968, two of which, Nos 34 and 35 (MCD 134/5F), were found at the council's depot on Lewes Road in 1980. The former has clearly been converted to open-top. (Les Flint)

Brighton Borough Transport turned to the Leyland Atlantean for its double-deck requirements in the mid-1970s. No. 60 (JFG 360N) was photographed at the town's railway station in the spring of 1983. This AN68/1R, delivered in 1975, had East Lancs seventy-three-seat bodywork, fitted with dual-doorway. Note that the fleet name is clearly 'Brighton Corporation', despite that organisation ceasing to exist before the bus was built!

For a short while Brighton Borough Transport adopted a rather garish colour scheme, as displayed on No. 29 (XFG 29Y), a forty-nine-seat Leyland National 2. It is seen at the Old Steine just after delivery in 1983.

The orange-and-white (and bits in between!) livery was also applied to Brighton Borough Transport No. 37 (AVS 903T), bought from Maidstone Borough Transport to operate between the railway station and the shopping area at Churchill Square. This rare Bedford JJL with Marshall bodywork is seen at the station in spring 1984.

Brighton Borough Transport No. 17 (OAP 17W), an East Lancs-bodied Dennis Dominator, was repainted into a version of the old tram livery in 1986. This seventy-five-seat bus was photographed in Hove in summer 1987, being pursued by the competition, a Brighton & Hove Bristol VR.

The principal bus operator in Dundee, Tayside Regional Council, bought this East Lancs-bodied Dennis Dominator new in 1981 as fleet number 281 (JSL 281X). By 1986 it had been sold to Brighton Borough Transport, and was photographed as No. 40 at the Old Steine, about to turn into North Street.

Unlike many operators, Brighton Borough Transport did not feel the need to buy vast numbers of minibuses. Nevertheless, it did use them for specific duties, branded as 'Brighton Bustler'. Seen close to the railway station in March 1989 is No. 61 (E461 CWV), a Renault S56 with twenty-six-seat Alexander bodywork.

Brighton Borough Transport also used smaller vehicles on tendered services it won in rural Sussex. One such bus was No. 97 (H909 SKW), a Renault S75 with a twenty-nine-seat Whittaker body. It was found, on a misty morning in early 1992, at East Grinstead railway station.

A sizeable batch of Leyland Lynx fifty-one-seat saloons was bought by Brighton Borough Transport. One of them, No. 46 (F546 LUF), was photographed in the summer sun of 1990, calling at Brighton's main railway station.

Brighton Borough Transport also purchased Plaxton-bodied Dennis Darts for single-deck duties. One of them, No. 80 (J980 JNJ), has a good load of passengers on its forty seats, as it waits for the traffic lights at the junction of North Street and Old Steine in March 1993. Later that year, Brighton Borough Transport sold its operations to Brighton & Hove.

The other municipal operator in Sussex was Eastbourne Corporation Transport. Unusually, this business only ever ran motorbuses (since 1903), never having had trams or trolleybuses. An example of a pre-war bus is preserved No. 12 (JK 8418), a 1939-built Leyland Lion LT9, with a Leyland thirty-two-seat body. It is seen at the former corporation depot during a rally in early 1986.

In 1975, Eastbourne Borough Transport (as it had been renamed) had this amazing survivor, an AEC Regal III built in 1950. The thirty-seat dual-purpose East Lancs-bodied bus, seen as No. 93 (AHC 911), was photographed in the depot yard. It has since been preserved.

Eastbourne Corporation Transport had a sizeable fleet of East Lancs-bodied AEC Regent V double-deck buses, one of which, No. 57 (HJK 157), was photographed in 1976, still lettered as a corporation vehicle. It is seen in the town centre, passing an illegally parked Fiat 500.

Here is a 1977 view of the depot yard. Closest to the camera is No. 78 (BJK 678D), an East Lancs-bodied Leyland PD2A/30, seating sixty passengers. It is still in Eastbourne Corporation Transport livery, while the Atlantean behind is branded as an 'EBT' (Eastbourne Borough Transport) vehicle.

One of the East Lancs-bodied Leyland PD2A/30 buses, No. 84 (DHC 784E), was converted to open-top for summer duties along Eastbourne's seafront. Painted in a special all-over blue livery, it is seen in the sun of July 1975, having been photographed by Les Flint.

The Daimler Roadliner was never a very successful type of rear-engined single-deck bus, and it came as no surprise to the photographer to find a 'NOT TO BE MOVED' notice prominently displayed on No. 90 (EJK 890F) in the depot yard in 1976. The forty-five-seat, dual-doorway bodywork was built by East Lancs.

Eastbourne Corporation Transport also bought some rear-engined Leyland Panthers, bodied by East Lancs, featuring two doors and forty-three seats. One of them, No. 10 (HHC 910J), was photographed on Cornfield Road in the town centre, *c.* 1975. After withdrawal, this bus saw further service in Sussex with the Bexhill Bus Company.

Very much a standard bus with Eastbourne Borough Transport was No. 35 (YJK 935V), seen on Terminus Road in the town centre, in 1981. This Leyland Atlantean AN68A/2R with eighty-two-seat East Lancs bodywork, wearing an all-over advert, was one of several new in 1979.

A unique bus in the Eastbourne fleet was No. 94 (MJK 94L), a little Seddon Pennine 4, with twenty-five coach seats in a Seddon body. It is seen at the depot in 1975. Two years later it was sold to Cardiff City Transport.

1981 and 1982 saw Eastbourne Borough Transport purchase a batch of Dennis Dominators, all with East Lancs bodywork. No 38 (MPN 138W) was found in 1981 loading up on Terminus Road in the town centre, a thoroughfare that has long doubled as the town's bus station.

In 1988 Eastbourne Borough Transport bought a few Leyland Olympians for their double-deck requirements. No. 54 (E854 DPN), bodied by Northern Counties, was one, looking very similar to those purchased by Bexleybus in South East London. It was photographed in Terminus Road in March 1989, with the town's classic railway station in the left background. E854 DPN was later sold to East Yorkshire Motor Services, then on to Shamrock in South Wales.

Eastbourne Borough Transport was not averse to buying second-hand vehicles, including this Leyland National that had been new to London Country as No. SNB262. It is seen here, in Terminus Road, Eastbourne, in its new guise as No. 14 (NPK 262R), in late 1990. By that time, 'Eastbourne Buses' had become the new fleet name.

An unusual saloon purchased in early 1992 by Eastbourne Borough Transport was No. 22 (J122 FUF), a Dennis Dart with forty-one-seat Wadham Stringer bodywork. It was photographed in Terminus Road in March 1993.

Eastbourne Borough Transport No. 11 (G911 RPN) was another rare vehicle to be found in a council-owned fleet. This Dennis Javelin with Duple 300 bodywork, seating fifty-five passengers, was captured on film in Terminus Road in the summer of 1995. It had been new to the business in 1989.

Even more unusual in the Eastbourne Borough Transport fleet was No. 67 (JWF 47W), seen in Terminus Road in summer 1995. It had been new in 1980 to Limebourne of London, who had used this Roe-bodied Leyland Atlantean AN68/1R on sightseeing duties in the capital.

1997 saw the delivery of one of Eastbourne Borough Transport's first low-floor buses, Optare Excel No. 38 (R206 DKG). This forty-two-seat bus is seen passing the fine railway station frontage as it enters Terminus Road in March 2003.

Eastbourne Buses No. 52 (GX02 WXU), a low-floor DAF SB120 saloon with Wright 'Cadet' thirty-four-seat bodywork, was photographed loading up in Terminus Road in March 2003. This vehicle survived the Stagecoach takeover to become No. 35903 in 2008.

In the later years of Eastbourne Buses, several services were operated outside the borough's boundary. Fleet number 272 (R872 MDY) was found on 25 June 2006 departing from the small bus station in Uckfield. This seventy-seven-seat Optare Spectra double-decker had been new to the business in 1998.

One of the last vehicles new to Eastbourne Buses was No. 64 (AE06 XRS), a MAN 14.220 with MCV 'Evolution' bodywork seating forty passengers. It was photographed in Terminus Road on 24 April 2007, less than a year before Eastbourne Buses sold out to the Stagecoach Group. AE06 XRS became No. 39634 in that fleet, but was later exported to Malta.

Top Line was a joint operation between Eastbourne Borough Transport and Southdown, running competitive services in the Hastings area between 1987 and 1989. Operating one of these is MOD 822P, a Leyland National that had been new to Western National in 1976. It is seen in Hastings town centre in March 1989. In 1989 both Top Line and Hastings & District passed to Stagecoach.

Arriva has a small presence in West Sussex as a result of having taken over part of the Alder Valley business. At Horsham's tiny bus station in late 1998 is No. 154 (K154 BRF), a Dormobile-bodied Mercedes 709D. It had been new to Stevenson's of Uttoxeter and was transferred to Arriva's Scottish operation not long after this photograph was taken.

In Horsham town centre on 3 August 2006 we see Arriva No. 3069 (P269 FPK). This 1997-built Dennis Dart SLF/Plaxton thirty-nine-seat saloon had originally been in the Guildford & West Surrey fleet of British Bus.

Inherited from the Alder Valley fleet was Arriva's No. 5801 (F571 SMG), an Alexander-bodied Leyland Olympian. It was photographed at the very edge of its operating territory, at Haywards Heath, on 23 April 2007.

Arriva, having taken over the Kentish operations of Maidstone & District, also make an occasional visit into Brighton by virtue of their joint operation of route 729 from Tunbridge Wells. Seen not far its destination in March 2003 as it turns into North Street in Brighton is No. 5907 (K907 SKR). This Northern Counties-bodied Leyland Olympian had been new to Maidstone & District in early 1993.

Metrobus began life in 1983, running buses around Orpington in South East London and Kent. Gradual expansion saw it reach other parts and, in the autumn of 1997, one of the company's buses, WYW 78T, was found close to the railway station in Brighton. Confusingly, it *is* a Metrobus, built by MCW. It had been new to London Transport, where it had been given the fleet number M76.

The year 1999 saw Metrobus being taken over by the Go-Ahead Group. Today the company has a major presence in Sussex, running most of the services around Crawley and venturing further afield. No. 291 (W791 VMV), a twenty-nine-seat Dennis Dart SLF/Plaxton, was photographed on East Grinstead's high street in March 2002.

Another Dennis Dart SLF in the Metrobus fleet, this time with Caetano thirty-eight-seat bodywork, is seen among the modern buildings of Crawley New Town in March 2003. No. 363 (Y363 HMY) had been new to the company two years earlier.

An unusual vehicle in the Metrobus fleet was No. 158 (L58 UNS). This Volvo B10B-58 with Alexander 'Strider' bodywork had been new to Scottish independent Whitelaw of Stonehouse. It was photographed at Horsham's Carfax on 3 August 2006, prior to a trip to the coast.

Metrobus's 'Fastway' services were introduced in the early twenty-first century to provide bus rapid transit between Crawley and Gatwick Airport. A short section of guided busway is provided and the small guide wheels required for this are clearly seen on No. 548 (YN05 HCD) as it enters Crawley bus station on 22 February 2008. This all-Scania N94UB features a dual-doorway body capable of seating thirty-seven passengers.

Metrobus have introduced a smart new livery for buses working the 270 route between Brighton and East Grinstead. This is seen applied to No. 6782 (YY15 GDE), a thirty-eight-seat Alexander Dennis Enviro saloon, photographed on 5 May 2017 setting out from Brighton city centre. Brighton and Hove achieved city status in 2001.

In the early 1990s, having taken over Southdown, the Stagecoach Group attempted its first services in Eastbourne, using an unusual adaptation of the striped livery and the fleet name Eastbourne & District. Seen in those colours is No. 34 (PCD 80R), a Leyland National from the main fleet, photographed in Terminus Road, Eastbourne, in late 1990. Eastbourne & District, as a separate entity, did not last long.

In 1989 Stagecoach purchased the former Hastings & District operations and vehicles, including No. 407 (PVT 207L), which is seen inside Rye depot in March 1993, still in the last Hastings Buses livery. This Bristol RESL6L/ECW saloon had been new as No. 207 in the Potteries Motor Traction fleet. Alongside is ex-Eastbourne Leyland Atlantean RHC 727S.

Still wearing its Hastings Buses colour scheme, but with Stagecoach logos, is No. 271 (OWE 271K), a most unusual vehicle indeed. This Bristol VRT/SL6G with East Lancs bodywork had been new in 1972 to Sheffield Transport, later passing through the hands of South Yorkshire Passenger Transport Executive and, in 1979, Maidstone & District. It was photographed at Hastings railway station in summer 1992. Fortunately, it was bought for preservation the following year and has since been restored to its original condition.

One of the first double-deck buses purchased by Stagecoach for its former Southdown operations (taken over in 1989) was No. 710 (G710 TCD). Very much a standard vehicle of its time, it is seen looking bright at Lewes on a rainy day in 1990, not long after delivery. Lewes depot, seen behind, was later sold to Brighton & Hove, and has since closed.

Stagecoach South Coast Buses is the fleet name displayed on Leyland National No. 113 (ENJ 913V), which had been new to Southdown in 1979. Still looking very smart, it was photographed on a beautiful autumn day in 1995 on North Street in Brighton, heading for Eastbourne. In 2005, the Stagecoach services east of Brighton, including Lewes and Uckfield depots (but not the Hastings operations), were sold to Brighton & Hove.

Stagecoach returned to Eastbourne in a big way in December 2008 when Eastbourne Buses was purchased, having previously been an 'arm's length' company owned by the local council. One of the vehicles acquired from that source was No. 35901 (GX02 WXS), a Wright-bodied DAF saloon, seating thirty-four passengers. It had been numbered 50 by its previous owners and is seen on Terminus Road in the town on 5 February 2009.

As we have already seen, Maidstone & District's Hastings operations, after having been independent for a while, eventually passed to Stagecoach. It was a nice touch, then, that in 2005 No. 20654 (R654 HCD) lost its Stagecoach stripes in favour of a version of the old Maidstone colours to celebrate 100 years of public transport in Hastings. No. 20654 kept this livery for a good while and the Plaxton Paladin-bodied Volvo B10M-55 was photographed in Eastbourne on 23 April 2007.

Stagecoach's flagship services along the South Coast, ranging between Dover and Eastbourne, are branded as 'The Wave', and include routes 99 to 102. Modern Alexander Dennis Enviro double-deckers are employed on these services, an example being No. 10712 (SN66 VWA). It is seen in Rye on route 100, while sister vehicle No. 10702 (SN66 VVO) is operating service 100 on 11 April 2017.

It should not be forgotten that Stagecoach still has a major presence in West Sussex, having taken over the Southdown operations in that area. To illustrate these, we see No. 34520 (GX04 EXP) on a short working of the 700 service, which runs from Brighton to Portsmouth, in Shoreham-by-Sea, passing the Bridge Inn on 14 September 2009. This Dennis Dart SLF/Plaxton thirty-eight-seat bus had been new to the company in 2004.

At one time, Tillingbourne was one of the largest independent bus companies in the South East. Based in Surrey, their buses could be found in West Sussex, particularly in Horsham, where we see R203 YOR, a Mercedes-Benz 0405 with Optare Prisma forty-nine-seat bodywork. It had been new to the company in 1997 and was photographed a year later. Tillingbourne was closed down in 2001 and R203 YOR moved up north, to Black Prince of Morley, near Leeds.

Bexhill Town Bus Services (Manxtree) was set up in 1980 to operate services in the town abandoned by Maidstone & District. New legislation (the Transport Act 1980) had made this process a lot easier. Seen on one such duty is UCO 33L, a former Plymouth Leyland National, photographed at its seafront terminal in Bexhill-on-Sea in 1981. In later years, Renown took over the services.

Vernon's Coaches, based in Hailsham, East Sussex, was a short-lived operator that ran a stage carriage service into Eastbourne. It is there, in Terminus Road, that we see TWX 194L, which is about to depart for the small town of Heathfield in March 1986. This Bristol RELL6G/ECW bus had been new to the West Yorkshire Road Car Company in 1972.

Rambler Coaches of Hastings was founded in 1924 and still trades today. Most of the company's business is based on coaching activities, but a few bus routes have been operated over the years. At the time of writing, free bus services to a Tesco supermarket are advertised. Back in March 1989, No. 52 (WNH 52W), a former United Counties Bedford YMQ with thirty-three-seat Lex bodywork, was photographed in central Hastings on a working to Hollington, a suburb of the town.

An independent that is no longer with us is Wealden Beeline, based in the Kentish village of Five Oak Green. Seen in Eastbourne in summer 1995 is HEF 379N. This Leyland Leopard with Plaxton Elite Express coachwork had been new to Cleveland Transit in 1975. Wealden Beeline later succumbed to the might of Maidstone & District.

For a few years, a London/Essex operator, Blue Triangle, ran a regular stage service along the Sussex coast between Brighton and Eastbourne. It is in the latter town, in summer 1995, that we see BCD 819L, a former Southdown Leyland National, loading up on Terminus Road prior to departure for Brighton.

Later in 1995, Blue Triangle No. D52 (MHR 52X) was photographed in central Brighton, heading for East Saltdean. This Dennis Dominator with Northern Counties bodywork had been new to Thamesdown (formerly Swindon Corporation) in 1982. Blue Triangle's services in Sussex did not last long, but the London services continued and Blue Triangle became part of the Go-Ahead Group.

The seaside town of Worthing was once home to Cedar Travel, who used minibuses on a few local services. Found in the town on a wet day in March 1989 was D917 XUF, a VW LT55/Optare City Pacer with twenty-five coach seats. It had been new to the company in 1987.

Today, RDH Services have a smart fleet of coaches on private hire and schools duties, but at one time also ran several stage carriage routes in the area around Lewes and Haywards Heath. At the latter location, in November 2005, we see K430 OKH, a Dennis Dart/Plaxton bus, which was new to London Transport as No. DRL30. In 2009, RDH Services sold the bus routes to Countryliner.

L. J. Edwards of Hailsham once operated the 'Hailsham Town Bus' service using this Mercedes-Benz L609D with sixteen-seat Robin Hood bodywork, registered F740 RBK. It was photographed in Hailsham town centre in 1991. Today, similar services are in the hands of Cuckmere Buses.

The Cuckmere Community Bus was established in 1976 as a voluntary organisation running minibuses on local routes in the Cuckmere Valley and beyond. Gradually, the organisation has expanded, and was presented with the Queens Award for Voluntary Services. One of the minibuses, M141 CWV, is seen passing Eastbourne railway station in March 2003. This Mercedes-Benz L609D with sixteen seats in a Devon Conversions body had been new in 1995 and was sold in 2007.

Sussex Bus was another short-lived operator in the county, running services based in Chichester. Used on these routes was XSU 682, photographed at the bus station in the early 1990s. The chassis had previously been under a Plaxton coach body, owned by Smith of Garnswllt, South Wales, and registered OKG 158M. In 1990 it was given a Willowbrook Warrior forty-eight-seat body.

G646 DBG was a CVE Omni minibus new to C&M of Aintree in 1989. By the autumn of 1995 it had migrated to Sussex Bus, and was photographed passing the Stagecoach depot in Chester. Not long after, Sussex Bus was purchased by Stagecoach.

The Sussex Bus (not to be confused with Sussex Bus on the previous page) ran a fleet of red-liveried buses in the area north of Brighton, commencing in 2012. Dennis Dart SLF/Plaxton X236 WNO, new to Selkent in London, is seen at Churchill Square, Brighton, on 15 August 2013. Thanks to Trevor Hall for allowing use of this photograph.

PO58 KRD had been new to Kent County Council for its Park & Ride services in Kent. On 22 April 2015, when photographed in Brighton, at Castle Square, North Street (by Steven Hughes and used with permission), the Volvo B7RLE/Optare bus had passed to The Sussex Bus. Sadly, on 1 October 2016, the company's services (but not the vehicles) passed to Compass Travel.

Countryliner was originally the coaching arm of Drawlane's London & Country fleet, but was later sold by Arriva in a management buyout. By 2001 the company had started bus operations, mainly in Surrey, but later expansion saw Countryliner enter Sussex, having purchased routes from RDH Services. On 16 April 2007, P425 VRG, an ex-Go Northern Optare Metrorider, was found on services opposite Lewes bus station.

New to Countryliner in 2007, MAN 12.220/MCV thirty-five-seat bus AE07 DZD was photographed on Valentine's Day in Haywards Heath. Countryliner's Sussex services ceased in 2012 after financial difficulties. Route 40 from Cuckfield to Brighton, which AE07 DZD is operating, later passed to The Sussex Bus.

Coastal Buses ran a considerable network of bus routes in East Sussex from a base at Newick in the early years of the current century. Two of the company's buses are seen at Rye station approach in October 2005. Closest to the camera is GU52 HKC, a Plaxton-bodied Dennis Dart SLF. It had been bought new by the company, like the sister vehicle behind. Coastal Buses has since ceased trading.

French-owned Connex once had the franchises to operated trains over the South Central area, including the line to Uckfield. That railway had once extended to Lewes. For a short while the company ran a connecting bus service, using this twenty-nine-seat Dennis Dart SLF/ Plaxton bus, registered W363 ABD. It was photographed at Uckfield station in the summer of 2000, awaiting departure.

A most unusual bus operation is that of a Brighton-based concern, Big Lemon. The company has mainly run minibuses, but on 8 October 2007 M451 LLJ was found in central Brighton. This Dennis Dart with East Lancs bodywork had been new to Bournemouth Transport. At the time of writing, Big Lemon is planning to introduce solar-powered vehicles onto its services.

A relative newcomer to the East Sussex bus scene is Seaford & District. The company's most high-profile operation is running open-top buses for tourists in Eastbourne, but some stage carriage work has been undertaken, though most of that has now been given up. On 5 May 2017 Dennis Dart SLF/Plaxton Pointer bus SFZ 454 is seen on Terminus Road in Eastbourne. This bus had been new to Metroline in London, registered Y658 NLO.

Not to be confused with the original Southdown company, Southdown PSV today operates several bus routes in the West Sussex area. On one of those duties is the Alexander Dennis Enviro 200 thirty-seven-seat saloon, registered GX57 BXH, seen arriving at Crawley bus station on 20 February 2008.

Emsworth & District is an independent bus company based at Southbourne in West Sussex, though Emsworth itself is actually in Hampshire. On 4 February 2008, H37 YCW was photographed on West Street in Chichester, close to the cathedral. This unusual Leyland Swift with bodywork by Reeve Burgess had been new to Hyndburn Transport, Accrington, in 1990.

Another company based in West Sussex, at Durrington near Worthing, is Compass Travel, now running a considerable mileage throughout Sussex and beyond. At Horsham on 3 August 2006, twenty-nine-seat Dennis Dart SLF/Plaxton GX54 AWH was photographed on service arriving at its Carfax departure point.

Renown Travel was established in the 1960s, but it did not commence bus service operation until the 1980s. The headquarters of the company are at Bexhill-on-Sea and most of the company's bus routes are close to the coast. Seen in Newhaven on 19 October 2007 is ANZ 8799. This Carlyle-bodied Dennis Dart had been given a modified Plaxton Pointer front end, giving it an unusual appearance. It had originally been registered H167 NON and had been new to London Buses as No. DT167.

Renown Travel sold its Eastbourne operations to Stagecoach in 2009, but today still runs services around the Kent and East Sussex borders. At Rye on 11 April 2017 we see No. 11 (SN53 AVC), a former Lothian Buses Transbus Dart SLF with Scarborough-built bodywork.

Southern Transit, based near Shoreham-by-Sea, does have a small amount of stage carriage work, but concentrates on engineering and railway replacement work. On such a duty, at the east side of Brighton station, on 26 April 2009 is F807 YLV. This MCW Mark II Metrobus had been new to Merseyside PTE in 1989.

Britain's major airports have long been full of interest for bus enthusiasts and Gatwick is no exception. This National Cark Parks-owned Leyland National 2 thirty-one-seat, dual-doored bus, OGN 877Y, was found at the terminal's main bus stand in spring 1984, less than a year after its delivery.

Also on car park duties is the Airlinks-owned X833 NWX, a DAF SB220/East Lancs B29D bus, new to the company in 2000. It was photographed in a layby outside the main terminal at Gatwick on a sunny day in March 2003.